Beginning With
BUDGIES

By Anne Ray Streeter

Photographs by Wayne Wallace, except as follows: Dr. Herbert R. Axelrod, 109. Kerry Donnelly, 105 top. Michael Gilroy, 16-17, 77, 80-81. Friedrich Goethe, 107. Ray Hanson, 63 top. Harry V. Lacey, title page, 29, 87, 99, 111, 117, 123. Bruce D. Lavoy, 57 bottom. Louise Van der Meid, 48-49, 67, 75, 105 bottom. Norma Veitch, 57 top. Courtesy of Vogelpark Walsrode, 113. Matthew Vriends, 63 bottom.

Distributed in the UNITED STATES by T.F.H. Publications, Inc., 211 West Sylvania Avenue, Neptune City, NJ 07753; in CANADA by H & L Pet Supplies Inc., 27 Kingston Crescent, Kitchener, Ontario N2B 2T6; Rolf C. Hagen Ltd., 3225 Sartelon Street, Montreal 382 Quebec; in ENGLAND by T.F.H. Publications Limited, 4 Kier Park, Ascot, Berkshire SL5 7DS; in AUSTRALIA AND THE SOUTH PACIFIC by T.F.H. (Australia) Pty. Ltd., Box 149, Brookvale 2100 N.S.W., Australia; in NEW ZEALAND by Ross Haines & Son, Ltd., 18 Monmouth Street, Grey Lynn, Auckland 2 New Zealand; in SINGAPORE AND MALAYSIA by MPH Distributors (S) Pte., Ltd., 601 Sims Drive, # 03/07/21, Singapore 1438; in the PHILIPPINES by Bio-Research, 5 Lippay Street, San Lorenzo Village, Makati Rizal; in SOUTH AFRICA by Multipet Pty. Ltd., 30 Turners Avenue, Durban 4001. Published by T.F.H. Publications Inc. Manufactured in the United States of America by T.F.H. Publications, Inc.

Contents

Foreword

When I was a little girl, we had a little green parakeet named "Lani." I don't remember much about her. Nor do I remember well the several other parakeets my family attempted to raise. I do remember the cats using their seemingly endless ingenuity to get to these birds, eventually succeeding in killing the birds or helping them escape to who knows where.

With these memories entrenched in my mind, I'd never been drawn to parakeets as pets.

It wasn't until I was offered the opportunity to research and write this guide to caring for parakeets—or budgerigars as they're more properly called and the term I shall use most of the time—that I discovered how wonderfully affectionate and smart these little birds are.

I'm not a true expert on caring for budgerigars (or budgies, as they're sometimes referred to), but the publishers felt that as a long-time journalist I would seek the answers to questions most people would ask about buying and owning a budgerigar and then put those answers into an easily readable form.

In accepting the assignment, I promptly went out and talked with area pet store operators, bird breeders, veterinarians and other bird owners. I read several books on budgerigars and parrots found at pet stores and the local library.

Then I bought my budgerigar—a two-month-old lutino (yellow-colored) fancy variety that my son promptly named "Tweetie Bird." She appeared to be a female, but sexing these small creatures at such a young age is no sure thing, as will be discussed later in the book.

Facing page: The author with one of her pet birds, a cockatiel named Pearl.

By following the directions of those with whom I talked, modifying their suggestions when necessary to comply with my bird's unique personality, Tweetie Bird quickly became a family pet. She spends hours out of her cage, usually perched on the shoulder of some member of the family. She enjoys our company and keeps us entertained with her precocious personality and her cheerful chirps and chatters.

She has become such a favorite pet that I find it difficult to pass by a pet store without wanting to buy another of these adorable creatures.

I was warned by aviculturist John Smithers when he sold me Tweetie that this might be the case. It seems that he and Joe Pigeon—co-owners of *Birds of Paradise* pet store in Key West, Florida—started their love for birds with a single budgerigar. Within a few years they had 200 birds in their apartment, which led to the decision to open their pet store.

If you are buying your first pet bird, don't be surprised if the urge hits to expand your collection. But also keep in mind that a budgerigar makes a better pet if it is kept by itself, as will also be discussed later in the book.

The information in this book is geared for people like me who are interested primarily in having budgies as pets, perhaps also breeding or showing them as a hobby. For those who are primarily interested in breeding, genetics and exhibiting birds, there are more detailed books available at pet stores.

Recommendations on caring for these parakeets was provided by the following persons in the Florida Keys: Joe Pigeon and John Smithers of *Birds of Paradise;* Madonna Stedman and Linda Wedzicha of *Pampered*

Facing page: Joe Pigeon, co-owner of Birds of Paradise in Key West, became a bird enthusiast after purchasing a budgerigar five years ago.

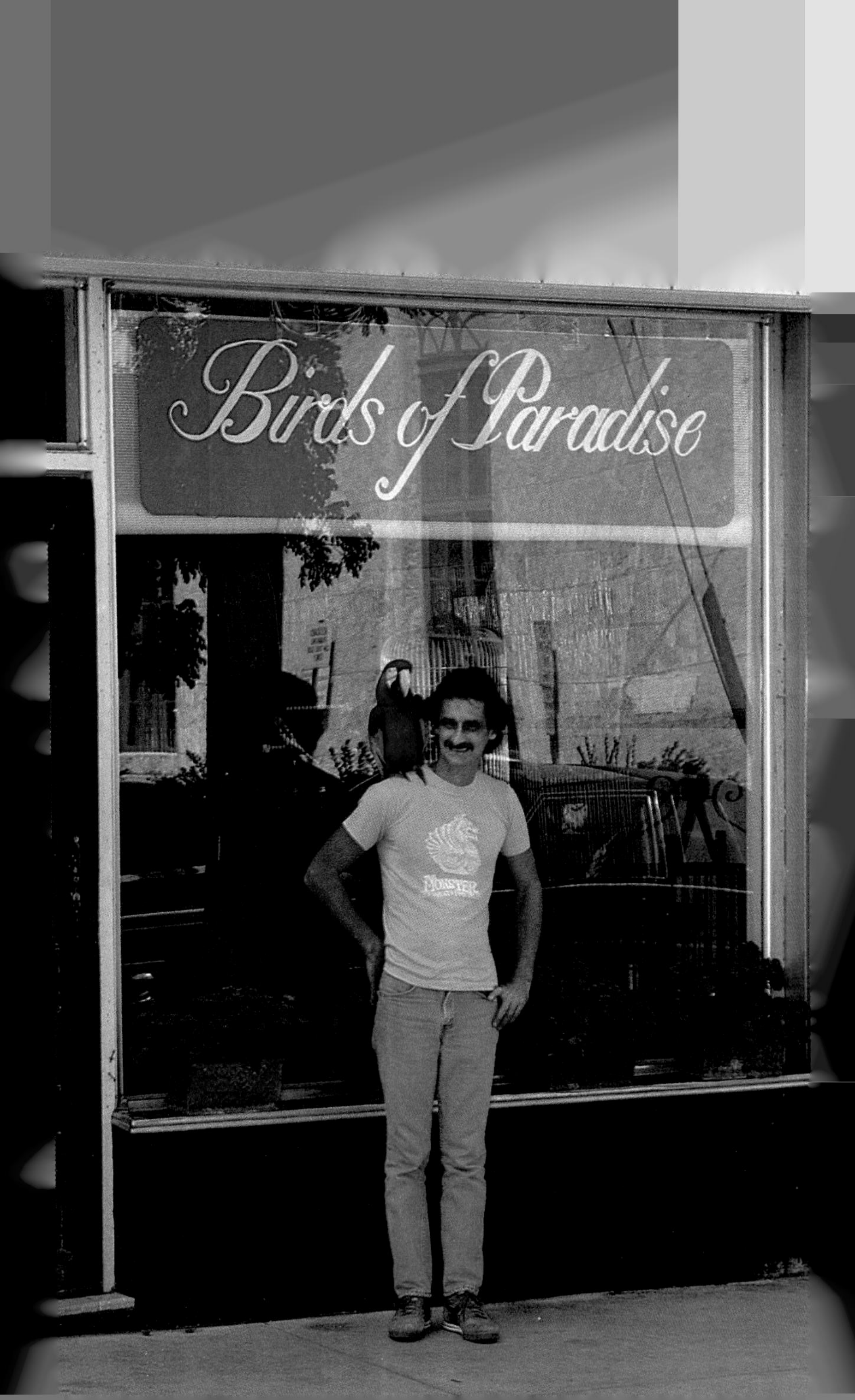
Birds of Paradise

Pets; Herb Martin, an avid breeder of all types of parrots; and Dr. Alan Bush, a veterinarian who specializes in birds. Their patience for my seemingly endless questions and their considerable knowledge has, I hope, made this book one that will provide you with the information necessary for truly enjoying the experience of caring for a budgerigar.

Why A Budgerigar?

It's no wonder the perky, petite parakeet—more properly called a budgerigar or "budgie"—has been one of the world's most popular cage birds for more than 100 years. It's the perfect pet for a child or for the adult wanting affectionate companionship. Additionally, because they take up little room and the cost of feeding is relatively little, they make a great pet for the elderly person or the person living alone. Their cheerful chattering and whistling are delightful company.

These colorful, gregarious Australian parrots are easy-to-tame and are capable of learning a wide vocabulary and selection of whistles if obtained at a young age (between two and six months old). They are hardy and with proper care have been known to live up to 15 years.

Whether alone or in a cage with other budgies, these small birds will amuse you with their chatter and their love of play. Give them any of the variety of toys made especially for budgies and they'll delight you with hours of animated antics.

If you want to breed birds for hobby or profit, the

Facing page: A budgerigar's yen for companionship makes it interested in the budgie in the mirror.

budgie is a prolific bird when matched with the right mate and in the right environment.

The price is attractive as well. Rather than spend hundreds of dollars for a larger member of the parrot family, the budgie can be purchased at a price ranging from about $10 to $20 for a basic bird to several times this depending on the color of its feathers. The less costly birds are the "normals"—those with the color of parakeets found in the wild, primarily the green- and yellow-feathered birds. The more expensive "fancy" birds can be any of a variety of colors, including the albino (white), lutino (yellow), and various shades and combinations of greens, blues, grays, yellows, violets and whites.

Longtime Favored Pet

The budgerigar has been a favorite pet bird for more than a century, dating to the days of explorers who discovered the colorful parrots in Australia.

Until the mid-19th century, only larger varieties of parrots had been brought to Europe by explorers to tropical lands where the colorful birds abounded. Only those who could afford the hefty price tag were able to enjoy the intelligence displayed by the various types of parrots available in Europe prior to the arrival of the budgerigar.

That changed when the colorful, petite budgie was brought from Australia to Europe. The hardy birds survived the long sea journey and were found to be prolific breeders. Once their reputation spread as a cage bird that

Facing page: Initially, no doubt, the popularity of budgies was a response to their beauty—only with time did their pet potential become known.

could be easily bred and taught to mimic words and phrases, they were in high demand.

Advantages of a Budgerigar

Bird lovers have long appreciated the advantages of having a budgie as a pet rather than the larger members of the parrot family. The bird is affordable. Its small size makes it easy to care for and easy to accommodate even in the smallest of apartments. It is a hardy bird with an average cage life span of four years.

If obtained at a young age (two to six months) budgies are easily tamed. They will sit on your finger or shoulder and most will even enjoy a gentle petting of their feathers. (My Tweetie Bird soon learned to sit on my shoulder, sometimes nestling under my hair, while I worked on my computer. My cockatiel sat on my other shoulder and their chatter back and forth kept me company.)

Easily Trained

Once tamed, with patience and care a budgie can learn to mimic melodic whistles and short phrases. But if you want your bird to learn how to "talk," postpone buying it a companion. If you place it in the same cage with another untrained parakeet, they'll devote their interest to each other and your attempts to teach either of them to "talk" will go unrewarded.

An exception to this, according to John Smithers, is

Facing page: A natural vivacity underlies a budgie's interest in toys and therefore its trainability.

when you place an untrained parakeet in a cage with one that's already learned how to mimic. In this situation, the younger bird will often learn to mimic words and phrases from the example set by the older bird.

Easily Cared For

If you're looking for a relatively trouble-free pet, one that won't take away from your limited leisure time, the parakeet is your best bet. With the proper cage (one that provides at minimum enough room for the bird to spread its wings), toys and plenty of perches and grillwork for climbing on, the budgie is at home.

Just spend about five minutes each day changing the bird's water and putting clean paper on the cage bottom. The food, provided there is enough seed in the dish (and not just empty hulls) and that it's clean, can be changed every other day. Just stir it up to make sure the bird can get to the fresh seed.

If you have to take a trip away from home, the bird can easily be cared for. Either have someone stop by daily to check on the bird or take the bird's cage to a friend's home where it will get attention.

There are five-day water dishes and covered seed dishes available at pet stores that enable a bird to go without care from its owner for a few days. However, it is generally recommended that these items not be used. Water and food can be dirtied by the bird's defecations and various harmful bacteria can grow in the water and in soft foods. A messy cage bottom can also result in illness.

Facing page: A bird's cage is its home. Appropriate furnishings and a suitable placement of the cage ensure its well-being. Many pet owners find that hanging the cage is the best choice in their homes.

Perhaps more importantly, a lonely bird is like a child. It's more likely to get into trouble by knocking over its dishes or injuring itself in some way. Tweetie Bird is a good example of this as she plays with her food dishes, literally moving them around the cage, emptying the water and seed along the way. Even if her dishes were secured, she'd find something equally mischievous to do with her cage. Five days without attention and Tweetie Bird would most likely be a sick or injured bird upon my return.

Of course, the more time you spend with your bird the more tame it will become, and part of having a pet is enjoying its company. These are sociable birds. In the wild, they fly in groups and spend hours preening each other and chattering away at each other. A single caged budgie instinctively craves the attention you give it.

If you can't be home, one pet store owner recommends leaving the radio on at a low volume. She suggested using tranquil classical music when the bird seems particularly anxious or nervous. Tweetie Bird chirps along with almost any music played and seems to enjoy the sounds of the television set nearby. Soothing baroque music seems to quiet down all of the animals of the household, which include Tweetie, a cockatiel kept in a separate cage, a cat and a dog. The minute I put that music on, they all retire to their individual cages or hiding places for a nap.

Variety of Ways to Care for Your Bird

One thing is certain about having a budgie for a

Overleaf: Some of the blue budgerigar varieties. Facing page, above: Singly kept budgies need affection from their owners. Below: Darkening the cage with a cover tells the bird it's time to quiet down and go to sleep.

pet—each bird has its own unique personality. Whatever advice is given to you by the pet store or breeder or whatever you read about caring for these birds, you'll have to tailor the recommendations to fit the needs and personality of your bird.

Each bird owner has his or her own methods of taming and training a bird, clipping its wings or nails, feeding the bird and caring for it when it's ill or injured. Each of their methods must have worked or they wouldn't be doing it. Some of their suggestions are included in the following pages of this book.

The key to success in caring for a parakeet or any bird is realizing that each bird is an individual and responds to various treatments in different ways. It may enjoy an apple or orange without coaxing or may just be satisfied with a well-balanced variety of seeds and grain supplemented with table food. Taming may come as quickly as the first 15 minutes of your relationship or it may require a few days of patient coaxing.

If you choose to breed your single cage bird, it may adapt readily to the selected mate and successfully produce young or it may require a setting similar to the wild where breeding takes place in colonies of birds, in which case you may need to buy and breed several parakeets.

Respect your bird. Learn its habits and, though it will usually adapt to your lifestyle, make sure you stay tuned in to its routine. If your bird's usual habits change suddenly—a change in eating or singing patterns, apathy, puffed up feathers or runny eyes and nose for example—check its environment to see if it's reacting to something new and stressful that can be quickly remedied or consider taking it to a veterinarian to see what's wrong.

Facing page: The eyes are helpful indicators of a bird's overall health: this youngster has a clear, open, alert eye.

With just a minimum of caring concern and love on your part, the budgerigar provides its owners with years of friendship filled with their precocious antics and affectionate manners.

What is a Budgerigar?

Melopsittacus undulatus, the parakeet or budgerigar, was known only to the Australian aborigines 200 years ago. They were a favored delicacy when removed from nest and fried over an open fire. The aborigines called the bird "bedgerigah" or "good to eat," which is where the English name budgerigar originated.

Although in the United States and some other areas of the world this bird is referred to as a "parakeet," it is more accurately called a budgerigar or budgie since there are many other small parrots also called parakeets.

Size and Color

The average budgie is about 6-8 inches in length from its beak to the tip of its tail. As a member of the parrot or "psittacine" order, it possesses the characteristic hooked beak, short neck and curious feet—two toes pointing forward and two pointing backward. Other members of the order include cockatiels (the second most popular pet parrot-family bird in the world), macaws, Amazon parrots, lovebirds and lories.

Facing page, above: Wild budgerigars are green; the blues are a mutant form that has been propagated in captivity. Below: The lighter edges of the wing coverts produce a wavy look, so that at one time budgies were called "undulated grass parakeets."

Commonly the adult budgie has a bright yellow face with the cheek feathers tipped with violet blue. There is a series of six black spots across its throat. Its upper part is colored with bars of black and yellow. Its underside from the lower neck to the beginning of the tail is bright green. The tail is long, with the largest tail feathers (those in the middle) colored a dark blue and the short outer feathers a light blue.

Its bill is yellowish in the adult bird and blackish in the immature bird. The cere (the fleshy part at the base of the beak where the nostrils are located) is typically blue except in the breeding female, when it turns chocolate brown.

In the young bird the colors are duller and the black spots on the throat are not clearly defined and may even be missing. There is noticeable barring of black lines across the forehead that fades with age.

Some pet store owners or breeders will try to determine the sex of a bird prior to its first molt (about three months) by the color of its cere. If the cere is a pinkish color, the bird may be a male. If it is bluish in color with white nostril margins, it could be a female. This method is not foolproof, and sexing young birds is extremely difficult. The intensity of the cere color varies among birds, and the color may pale in birds that are sick, stressed or molting.

Today's breeders have come up with many variations in colors, some of which also show up rarely in the wild, but these "oddly" colored birds are usually ignored by the other birds in their wild flock and their conspicuous coloration makes them an easy mark for their enemies. The variations in color will be discussed in the chapter headed *Breeding Budgies*.

Facing page: That these budgies are young is evident from the barring that extends back from the cere. Cere color, however, is quite variable at this age.

In the Wild

In its natural habitat in Australia, the budgerigar is a nomadic bird in constant search for seeds and water in the more arid central areas of that continent. Only in extreme droughts does the bird ever venture to the coastal areas.

This small, colorful bird has a penchant for small ripened seeds, preferring to eat early in the morning and in the late evening.

Its small size and determined flight enables the bird to fly great distances at quick speeds in search of seed and water. Its journey takes it over an estimated 70% of the continent, where it obtains nourishment from the grassy areas of the desert and semi-desert lands as well as from the pasture or grazing areas of the country.

The hardiness of the budgie has been demonstrated through research that indicates the bird can live on minimal amounts of water, extracting moisture from stems and leaves of plants and bushes if no other source is available. Domesticated birds have been known to live at least 38 days without water in temperatures of about 80°F. It is this ability that is credited with the budgie's survival of the long sea journey between Australia and Europe when the birds were first introduced to Europeans in the early 1800's.

In the wild, these birds withstand temperatures that range from 30°F to 100°F. In the extreme heat they use the coolness of the trees for protection, their green and yellow coloration enabling them to blend in with the color combination of green leaves and sunshine.

The budgie is a "colony" bird, meaning that it flies in

Facing page: In parrots, green serves as camouflage. Here, the cere color is that of a mature hen.

flocks that range in size   from 20 to 100 birds. During adverse conditions various flocks come together, offering greater protection for each other. Thousands of birds have reportedly darkened the sky in their flight in search of favorable conditions.

The budgerigar is an "opportunistic" breeder, meaning it can breed anytime the conditions are favorable. In the wild, the birds tend to lay fewer or no eggs at all during the winter when food is scarce.

They appear to have no particular preference for the type of tree they use for their nests, but it must have a proper size opening and it is usually in the vicinity of water. The budgie may even use logs on the ground or may burrow into the dirt among the roots of fallen trees for their nests.

The hen lays four to six eggs on alternate days. She is fed by the cock, and in turn, through regurgitation of the food, she feeds the young once they've hatched.

It is said that in the wild budgies have few predators. Their principal enemies are falcons and hawks. Just the sound of a falcon approaching is enough to silence a flock of budgies and send them off in frightened flight.

The bird's major enemy is nature herself—droughts, brushfires, thunderstorms and the like. In what is called Australia's "great bird holocaust" of 1932, extreme heat for 51 days in which the average shade temperature was 110°F caused the death of thousands of birds. Many were reportedly drowned when, spotting surface water, they swooped down for a drink, only to be pushed under by other birds piling in on top of them.

Facing page: As cavity nesters, budgies in captivity are bred in boxes, in which a board with a shallow depression serves to contain the eggs. Not all the eggs hatch at the same time, so nestlings often differ in age and therefore development.

Discovery and Domestication

The first illustration of budgies appeared in Shaw and Nodder's *Naturalists Miscellany* in 1805. In this book the bird is given the scientific name *Psittacus undulatus,* which means a parrot with undulating or diversified waves of color.

Naturalist John Gould, who went to Australia in the 1840's to compile books on the profusion of parrots and other birds, changed the name to *Melopsittacus undulatus*—"melo" meaning song.

The bird was known by a variety of names at the time, including zebra parrot, undulated parakeet, and shell parrot. A Scottish school teacher named William Gardner, who came to Australia to settle, wrote about the bird between the years of 1830 and 1852. He used the term "Budgerry Gaan," apparently the first written reference that resembles the name "budgerigar."

John Gould's fascination with the birds he encountered on his trip to Australia prompted him to collect and ship several specimens to England. The interest these birds received from breeders interested in raising the birds in captivity prompted several collecting expeditions to Australia. Though many of the birds did not survive the long days at sea and the new European climate, the budgie population in captivity began to grow as breeders found the proper foods and nesting environment. Commercial hatcheries developed in the late 19th century in Europe, particularly in the French region of Toulouse, where the mild climate was more suitable.

Facing page: A. F. Lydon's depiction of the budgerigar, done in the 1880s for Greene's *Parrots in Captivity.*

By the time the Australian government took measures to protect the dwindling numbers of budgies in the wild by stopping their exportation in the 1920's, bird fanciers had mastered successful breeding techniques.

The popularity of the colorful bird increased as word spread of its ability to mimic the human voice and whistles. The growing numbers of budgies bred in captivity reduced the cost of the bird, making them an affordable and popular household pet.

Today, bird farms in the United States are the main source of supply of budgies worldwide. Not only are the birds sold as pets, but they're a favorite with bird fanciers interested in the breeding of show birds. The interest in breeding ever-increasing varieties of colors, striving to produce a bird that meets the stringent showbird qualifications, has made the budgie a favorite for genetics research.

The Budgerigar as Pet

If all that's been said thus far about the budgie as the perfect pet appeals to you, ask yourself the following questions before racing out to buy one:

1) Do you or other family members have the time to spend in cultivating the friendship of this bird? A single caged budgie will depend on you for its companionship. It is a sociable bird, and if you don't have the time to talk and play with it, then perhaps you should consider buying another type of bird to keep it company.

2) Is the environment where the bird will be placed an appropriate one? If there are a lot of windows or drafts, special precautions will need to be taken to prevent your

Facing page: Even though a budgie is sociable by nature, a human being will need time and patience in order to acquire its trust.

bird from being chilled. If you have other pets, particularly a cat or dog, then the bird's cage will need to be placed out of reach, preferably hanging from the ceiling. Caution must be taken to keep doors and windows closed or screened to keep an out-of-cage bird from escaping. Young children must be instructed on how to treat the bird. A budgie can be easily injured by a groping youngster. Out of fear, an adult budgie can inflict a painful bite, particularly to a child, and this unnecessary situation should be avoided if proper care is taken.

3) Are you committed to being attentive to the bird's needs? Though the feeding and cleaning of a bird's cage takes hardly any time at all, it is of critical importance to the bird's health that this routine be conducted daily. Just as humans must eat and drink uncontaminated food from clean dishes to protect themselves from illness, so do birds. Harmful bacteria and molds can grow in damp food left too long in a bird's dish. The bird's droppings can contaminate the food and water supply. If the cage bottom is not covered with clean paper each day, the dried droppings can blow around, creating potential health hazards.

If the bird will be left alone for longer than a day or two, it is advisable to have someone check on it daily, or else you could take the bird in its cage to someone's home where the proper attention can be provided.

The commitment to pay attention to the bird means learning the budgie's habits so that when its routine suddenly changes, you'll be tuned in enough to know there's a problem that must be remedied in a hurry. A sick bird will fake normalcy as long as possible, reacting instinctively to the law of the wild where the weakest bird falls

Facing page, above: A cuttlebone provides nutrients and is also an outlet for a budgie's energy. Frequent cleaning of the cage tray is the best insurance against illness.

victim to its enemies. By the time the symptoms of illness can no longer be hidden by the bird, it's often too late for even the best of veterinarians to return the bird to good health.

4) After the initial investment of buying the bird, are you willing to spend what is necessary to provide an adequate cage, a well-balanced diet and medical attention? As with any pet, you must be committed to caring for it. It can't be just turned loose and expected to live a healthy life. Some of the costs involved include the price of a cage that is large enough for the budgie to spread its wings without touching the sides of the cage; a high-quality mixture of seeds and cereal grains as well as nutritional supplements that provide the necessary vitamins and minerals; and possible veterinarian fees, particularly if you follow the recommendation that a newly-purchased bird be taken for a physical exam followed by annual checkups to assure the bird is in good health.

5) What do you want the bird for? This is an important question, for the answer could determine whether you buy one or more birds, male or female. For example, if the budgie is to be a pet in the truest sense of the word, it is best to buy one bird so it will learn to focus its attention on you and other family members. A single caged bird may be trained to talk or whistle and will gladly sit on your finger or shoulder while you carry it as you go about your business.

Add another bird and, no matter how tame that first bird was, it is likely to turn its attention to its feathered friend. It will either teach the new friend all it knows or it will forget all those phrases and whistles learned after many patient hours of training.

Facing page: Many different cage designs are available. Be sure to choose one that not only looks attractive but is also easy to clean.

If breeding is the purpose of purchasing the bird, then of course you must also obtain a mate. And since budgies are community birds, they breed best when in the presence of other breeding budgies. This means you may have to have several birds, which leads to a need for an indoor or outdoor aviary especially constructed to accommodate breeding pairs. More on this is included in the section on breeding.

After considering these questions, if it is determined that a budgie is still the pet desired, then begins the search for the perfect companion.

Buying a Budgerigar

There are many ways of locating and buying a budgerigar. Perhaps the most common place to start is the local pet store, where you're likely to find someone qualified to answer any of the questions typically raised by a nervous new owner. Buying from a pet store assures that when you leave with your bird you'll also be well-equipped with the proper cage and other necessities. A reputable pet store will be there to answer questions about the bird once you get it home, particularly if, for some reason, the bird becomes ill in the first few days.

Another good source is a breeder, who will know exactly when the bird was born and can attest to its upbringing, thus assuring the bird did not spend its early days in a crowded cage with hundreds of other birds, some of which may have carried a potentially fatal disease.

Veterinarians are good to contact for they will most

Facing page, above: Anyone thinking of buying one of these birds will need to determine whether it is ill or just sleepy. Below: Pet shops offer livestock as well as all the accessories needed to keep them properly.

likely be able to recommend a good breeder or pet store reputed to have healthy birds. Ask friends who have birds for their advice. If there is a local bird club, attend a meeting to find out where they recommend purchasing your pet.

Most of these sources are listed in the phone book and some even run advertisements in the classified sections of the local newspaper, particularly when there's a recently hatched clutch that will soon be for sale.

Finding a Healthy Bird

When looking at potential budgies, it is important to check for certain signs that indicate a bird's health.

A healthy bird will be bright and alert. Don't be fooled into thinking that an apathetic bird is tame. It may be so sick that it does not care about any potential dangers.

On the other hand, a candidate for taming may stand out in the crowd of its cagemates by continuing to calmly perform its natural functions such as eating and preening itself even while being watched from outside the cage.

A bird with ruffled feathers and continually in a sleeping posture that is not easily aroused or one with a runny nose or eyes is also not a good bet. The plumage should be smooth and there should be no bare spots.

Have the salesperson check the breast of the parakeet to determine if it's plump and round rather than sharp or emaciated, indicating an unhealthy bird. It is also unwise

Facing page, above: Cages of this size are ample for single pets. Pairs can be bred in them too, provided a nest box is installed inside or out. Below: Budgies that exhibit alertness, curiosity, and little fear when one approaches the cage often make the best pets.

to buy a bird that has moist or caked wet droppings on the underside of its tail or whose droppings are not black and white and in good form—all possible indicators of an intestinal disease.

Respiration should not be labored and irregular but rather slow and even. Missing toes or claws are not a problem unless the wound is fresh or there's swelling in the area.

Determining Its Age

It is not always easy to tell the exact age of some birds, hence the need to be able to trust what the pet store owner, vet or breeder tells you about the bird. The age plays an important part in selection if the reason for having the bird is to tame and train it, making it into a lovable companion. Optimally, it is best to get the budgie at a very young age, preferably no older than two months, just as it's left the nest and is capable of cracking seed and feeding itself.

In most color variations of the budgie, the very young bird has more softly colored feathers than the adult, and most have distinctive zebra-type markings or barring on the tops of their heads. These black markings disappear after the first molt at about three months of age. The flecks of dark colors on their faces under their beaks are then replaced by six well-defined spots.

Another indication of age is the color of the bird's iris: black in most birds at a young age, encircled in white after about six months. If a bird has a distinctively blue or chocolate cere, then it is too old to buy for taming purposes.

Facing page: A blue bar-head enjoys a little freedom atop its cage. Note its eye color.

Determining Sex

Determining whether the bird you like is a male or a female can be difficult in a young bird, but if you want the bird to be a talker or more tame in nature, then you'll probably want a cock. Males have a better reputation for being friendlier and easier to work with. Again, a reputable bird fancier can help in selection of the proper sex.

One thing to look for in all but the white and yellow budgies is the color of the bird's cere. In the young male, the cere is pale blue and somewhat plump. The young female has a flatter and paler cere that has some white around the nostrils. The cere of a male becomes more blue as it ages, while the female's becomes a pale blue to gray color except when breeding, when it will turn a deep chocolate brown.

Another indicator of sex is the width of the area between the bird's pelvic bones, naturally wider in females to allow easy passage of the eggs. This was demonstrated to me by Madonna Stedman of *Pampered Pets,* who pointed out the narrowness of the male's pelvic region compared to the female's wider space. Also, by lightly blowing on the feathers around the genital area you can determine whether it's a cock or hen, according to Stedman. A female's feathers are more fluffy and finer. A male has fewer, larger feathers.

If you're not interested in taming the bird, but rather in breeding it, then buying an older bird where sex is easier to ascertain may be a good idea.

Facing page: Unbarred forehead, light iris, and darkening cere—these indicate an adult hen coming into breeding condition.

Tagged Birds

Some budgies will have a metal band around one of their legs bearing an identification number. If your bird has this tag, record its number for safekeeping. This makes it easier to identify your bird should it be caged with others, at the vet's for example, or if it is stolen or lost and found by a stranger.

Breeders such as Herb Martin are strong believers in tagging birds. That way, if any of his customers have a problem with the bird, he knows exactly which bird they're talking about and when it was hatched. After a bird is a year old, the tag may be the only way of determining the bird's age.

With some breeds of parrots, tagging is an indication of the bird's legal importation into the United States. Since there is a growing illegal black market in birds being smuggled into the country, tagging is important in discerning the bird's origin. However, that's not as important for the budgie since the bulk of the birds on the market today are raised in this country.

Taking Your Bird Home

Getting your bird home and settled into its new environment with a minimum of stress to the pet is very important. The bird should be transported in a covered cage or in the specially-made carrying boxes provided by most pet stores. Some pet stores may put birds into paper bags, but this could prove to be a bad idea if care is not

Facing page: If you purchase both budgie and cage at the same time and the distance that must be traveled is short, then the bird can be transported in a covered cage.

taken to keep the bird from being injured by someone sitting on the bag or placing a heavy object on top of it.

If it's a cold day, take special care to keep the bird warm, possibly postponing the trip if it's raining since the dampness could lead to a cold. If it's a warm day, however, be sure not to leave the bird in the car with the windows rolled up. The temperature outside of the car may be pleasant enough, but sunlight magnified by the vehicle's glass and metal construction could cause the interior to heat up like an oven, quickly killing the bird.

It is important to keep the bird covered on its way to its new home to protect it from wind and, perhaps more importantly, from the frightening array of strange sights and sounds. The less stress the better for the bird.

If at all possible, have the bird's new home—cage or aviary—ready for its new occupant before placing the budgie inside. Placing a bird into its new home and then putting all of the needed feeding utensils, toys and the like into the cage will only upset the bird unnecessarily.

As John Smithers says, the bird should be made to feel safe inside of its cage, as free from intruders as possible—including you.

Choosing the Proper Cage

Selecting the proper cage is extremely important. The pet store should have a wide selection of sizes and shapes and can recommend those cages that are best for the budgie. Just make sure the cage's design complies with the following guidelines:

1) A wide enough structure to allow the bird to stretch

Overleaf: The birds housed in these flights illustrate some of the different colors and markings found in budgerigars. Facing page: When transporting a bird, be sure to consider its sensitivity to temperature.

its wings without touching the sides of the cage. The ideal size is at least 2 feet in length with a height and width of no less than 1 foot. The bars should be spaced no farther apart than ½ inch and should be horizontal rather than vertical. This is so the bird can climb the sides of the cage—an important form of exercise for the caged bird.

Many thinner-wired cages that are more suitable for canaries and finches have vertical bars that keep budgies from exercising their climbing capabilities.

Some cages have built-in playgrounds on the inside of the cage door—when the door is opened outward, the bird has easy access to a ladder and swing. However, when the cage door is closed, the playground takes up too much of the available flight space. This is probably all right if your bird has clipped wings and thus cannot fly. Birds with limited flight have been known to exercise their wings while remaining stationary on their perch. But if your bird can fly and is in the cage most of the time, this playground arrangement is not advisable.

To aid in keeping empty seed hulls from being scattered outside of the cage, many cages have a plastic rim or shield about 2 inches high around the bottom of the cage. The seed dishes in these cages are below the plastic rim. If your cage doesn't have this rim, check with your pet store to see if they have in stock a specially made "bib" that will fit around your cage to keep the seed inside rather than out.

2) Appropriate heavy-wire parrot construction, preferably using stainless steel or other non-rusting metal. The more decorative cages made from bamboo or colored with toxic paints are not suitable for a budgie.

Facing page: Playgrounds offer budgies, like this lutino, opportunities for exercise and amusement.

They love to chew on the materials, eventually escaping from the wooden structure or being harmed by the paints. If building a cage, just be certain that non-toxic materials are used and that there are no sharp wires left exposed that might possibly injure the bird.

3) A bottom tray that can be pulled out for easy cleaning of the cage floor. Some cages have a wire grill across the tray that keeps the bird from walking in its own waste. My parakeet seems to like to be on the bottom of the floor where she can pull her food dish around and bury it under the paper toweling I use as the floor's cover. On the other hand, the grill floor works well with my cockatiel, a slightly larger parrot that has no problem walking on the wire bars and seems to have no interest on being on the floor, preferring instead the several perches in her cage.

4) A door large enough for you to put your hand in the cage and bring the bird out without touching any point. A small door only makes a bird more nervous about leaving the safety of its cage. Make sure the latch on the door can't be opened by an industrious budgie. Safety locks are available at the pet store to assure your bird stays in the cage out of harm's way until you want to bring it out. I learned this lesson the hard way when Tweetie opened her cage door and fell to the ground, only to be pounced on by my Doberman Pinscher pup. The results were a broken leg and an injured wing, not to mention an extremely frightened bird. More of what emergency actions were taken to save the bird will be covered in the section on caring for the sick and injured bird.

Facing page, above: Cages constructed so that the wire part can be lifted from the pan are very practical. In this model, a tray fits into the bottom of the pan. Below: Green foods add important nutrients to a budgie's diet.

Getting the Cage Ready

A properly furnished cage should include feed and water dishes that are easily accessible for daily attention. I prefer cages that provide separate doors through which the water and feed dishes can be refilled without having to place your hand into the bird's cage, disturbing the bird in the process. Other cages place the feeding dishes inside, necessitating actually reaching in. Some cages and food dishes have covers of a type that allow the bird access but protects the food and water from the bird's droppings. This is a good idea providing your bird isn't averse to eating from a sheltered container as some birds seem to be. In fact, some young birds may starve to death if covered dishes are used since they simply can't find the food.

Budgies love to play, particularly if they are alone in the cage. Thus any of a variety of bells and toys will keep them chattering away and contented for hours. But be careful with a very young bird that may get tangled up in a bell chain or toy, perhaps injuring itself. Also, be sure the toys provided have no loose parts or clangers that could be easily swallowed by the bird.

Mirrors are not suggested for the bird if you plan to teach it to talk since the bird will pay attention to its reflection instead of to you. But if you don't have time to spend with the bird, a mirror makes for a good companion substitute.

The cage should have plenty of perches of varying widths so that the bird can move about the cage and exercise its legs and feet. Natural woods with bark are great, as long as the wood is from a non-poisonous tree (check

Facing page, above: Perches and utensils for food and water are basic cage accessories: Below: Ladders, toys, and additional food cups can be added to suit the bird's needs and the owner's routine.

with your county agricultural extension office or pet store to be sure the plant you have in mind is suitable for a bird. Make sure the natural perch is washed thoroughly to remove any trace of insecticides.

A special toy for your bird is a fairly new product on the market called Nylabird. These chewable playthings give the bird something to gnaw on that will supply it with its nutritional requirement for calcium, keep it entertained and at the same time prevent its beak from getting too long. Your pet store or veterinarian can tell you more about Nylabird.

Where to Place the Cage

Before bringing the bird home, decide where to place the cage. Take heed of the following no-no's:

1) Keep it away from drafts and windows to keep the bird from getting chilled.

2) Don't place it in direct sunlight. It's all right to have some sun in the cage as long as the bird has a shaded area to go to as well. On very hot days, don't put it in front of a window where the sun's heat is magnified and can be a killer.

3) In areas where there are changes in the seasons, make sure your bird is placed in a temperature-controlled area the year around. Don't place it near an open-flame heater or right in front of a frigid air conditioner.

(Note: Keep in mind that in the wild these hardly little birds withstand temperature variations of between 30 and 100°F, but a bird that has been acclimated to more stable temperatures could be adversely affected by such changes.)

Facing page: Potential dangers to budgies are poisonous plants (poinsettia) that can be nibbled, and too much exposure to direct sunlight.

4) Don't place it near poisonous plants such as oleanders, poinsettias or philodendrons where it might nibble on a leaf or two.

5) Don't place it near the stove or in any place that could prove dangerous if the bird is out of its cage.

6) Keep it out of reach of other household pets, particularly cats and large dogs. Since cats are such ingenious animals when faced with the temptation of a feathered treat, it is best to hang the cage from the ceiling (away from ceiling fans). This assures there are no nearby areas for the cat to climb to reach the bird. If placed on a shelf, make sure the cat can't knock the cage down, which could result in an open cage door with a hungry cat ready to pounce on the disoriented bird.

As for dogs, make sure the dog is outside of the room when you bring your bird out. A playful dog can do tremendous damage to a bird just by simply placing its paw on top of it.

Please don't disregard this advice. When we brought Tweetie home, she had been in her cage on a book shelf for less than two hours when our cat managed to knock the cage to the floor and let the bird out. Fortunately, we got to the bird first and promptly moved the cage to a safer place—tied to a bookcase where she is inaccessible from any direction. We're now working on teaching Tweetie to say "I thought I saw a pussy cat." And, as mentioned before, our Dobie badly injured Tweetie when the bird got out of her cage. These birds depend on you for their protection. Don't let them down.

7) Place the bird out of reach of any young children who might unwittingly let the bird out when no one is around to protect it.

Facing page: Other house pets may be a threat to a pet budgie. Take care to observe how they respond to one another, and be sure to supervise them when the bird is out of its cage.

8) Don't put a single caged bird in a secluded area away from human contact. These birds are sociable by nature and deserve to be placed where they'll receive attention from family members.

9) A word of caution to personal computer users— don't place the cage where the bird is likely to drop seed hulls or spray water right onto your valuable equipment. An accidentally dropped water dish or seed tray could ruin a floppy disc or, even worse, cause irreparable damage to the computer keyboard, terminal or printer.

About Aviaries

It's been said that a cage can never be big enough for a bird. If you have the room and are planning to have additional birds for variety or for breeding purposes, then you'll need an aviary.

An indoor aviary can be set up just about anywhere as long as the same guidelines for placement of a cage are followed. Aviaries are easily made from wire mesh and wooden boards. The floor of the room may serve as the cage bottom, with a low-placed door included for ease in cleaning. Food dishes should be placed on a shelf halfway up the wall within easy reach of all the birds.

Outdoor aviaries are preferable since there is usually more room for flight and the birds benefit from the natural elements such as sun and fresh air.

The most important factor in building either an indoor or outdoor aviary is assuring the length of the cage is long enough to provide the longest possible flying

Facing page: Simple budgerigar aviaries constructed of wood and wire mesh. Budgies are often more prolific when housed in colonies.

distance. Perches and feeding dishes should be placed only toward the top and bottom of the aviary in order to not interfere with the flight path of the birds. A "stepping" arrangement of perches in one area of the aviary enables the birds to congregate as they would in the wild.

The outdoor aviary may be built on either a concrete or soil floor. A concrete foundation that is embedded one to two feet below ground and extends as high as possible above ground is preferable since it discourages rats, mice, snakes and other predators. It is also easier to clean.

Some soil on top of the concrete appeals to birds that prefer walking on the dirt rather than concrete. It also enables you to sprinkle bird seed in the soil, which then sprouts into the budgies' favorite treats—sprouted seeds.

The aviary itself should be constructed from galvanized iron pipes, frames that have been coated with a non-toxic rust-proof paint or else made from a hardwood such as eucalyptus. Don't use a softer wood since, as mentioned before, budgies can chew through the wood to escape. A fine wire mesh—as small a mesh as possible to keep unwanted "critters" out—should be used, with a double layer on the roof to provide further protection to the birds.

There should be a sheltered area attached that may be made from bricks, wood or manufactured sheeting. This area should be easily accessible to the birds and should be bright and well-insulated. By splitting the facility into at least two separate flight paths, the cocks and hens can be separated when breeding has been suspended or when there is the need to isolate a sick or injured bird.

The birds like to congregate in their indoor shelter on

Facing page: A bird cage should not be situated near a fan or near a stove because of the potential dangers of drafts, overheating, and accidental injuries.

Since 1952, *Tropical Fish Hobbyist* has been the source of accurate, up-to-the-minute, and fascinating information on every facet of the aquarium hobby. Join the more than 50,000 devoted readers world-wide who wouldn't miss a single issue.

Subscribe right now so you don't miss a single copy!

...From T.F.H., the world's largest publisher of bird books, a new bird magazine for birdkeepers all over the world...

CAGED BIRD HOBBYIST
IS FOR EVERYONE
WHO LOVES BIRDS.

CAGED BIRD HOBBYIST
IS PACKED WITH VALUABLE
INFORMATION SHOWING HOW
TO FEED, HOUSE, TRAIN AND CARE
FOR ALL TYPES OF BIRDS.

Subscribe right now so you don't miss a single copy!   SM-316

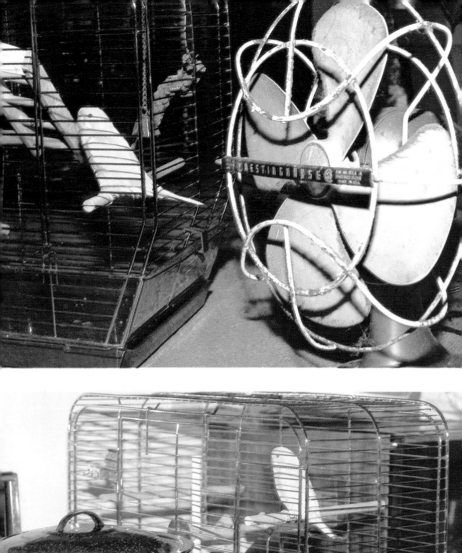

wet, cold days or when the sun is at its hottest, using the outdoor aviary early in the mornings and in the early evenings.

Again, the interior doorways that allow access to both the outdoor and indoor aviary should be kept fairly low to prevent birds from escaping when you enter. Double doors protect the birds even further. Preparing the cage or aviary for nesting will be discussed in the section on breeding.

Free-Flying Birds

Some parakeet fanciers allow their pet birds to fly about the house with unclipped wings for long periods of time. My sister's family had a budgie named "Ranger" that was always out of its cage. In general, a budgie seems to prefer young children to adults if a choice presents itself. This trait was exemplified by Ranger, who would sit on the head of my sister's son while he brushed his teeth or on his shoulder while doing homework.

Ranger would even join the family at the dinner table, nibbling the food on my nephew's plate. Ranger was definitely part of the family. It was a very sad day when the family discovered that the neighbor's cat had gotten into the house and had killed the poor bird.

Allowing your bird to fly free as did Ranger is fine, as long as all measures are taken to protect the bird from escaping or from being injured.

Facing page: In this flight (a large enclosure that allows the birds considerable room for flying), branches have been installed for perching.

Caring For the Bird

Too often, novice bird fanciers buy their first bird from an unreliable source ill-qualified to provide accurate information on caring for their bird. They leave with a sack of cheap bird seed in hand, thinking that's all their new friend will need for nourishment.

"That's like giving a child a store full of bakery goods like donuts and cakes—that kind of a diet would only lead to malnourishment and most likely death," warns Florida Keys veterinarian Alan Bush, who is also a bird fancier.

To make sure the bird is healthy and that you understand the importance of caring properly for the bird, Bush recommends making an appointment with a veterinarian who has some experience with birds. Wait a few days after bringing the bird home to give it a chance to get used to its new environment, however.

Most vets will give the bird a physical examination and will check its droppings to see if they're as firm and properly colored as they should be (a bull's-eye shape with black center and white outside). Some, like Dr. Bush, have literature and short film strips available to provide you with concise, easy to understand techniques on all aspects of caring for your bird.

It's a good idea to establish a relationship with a vet in the early stages of having your new pet so that if your bird does get sick you'll have a ready source of assistance. It is also advisable that the bird be taken for annual checkups.

Facing page: Taking a new pet budgie to a veterinarian for a checkup is a wise preventive measure.

Nutritional Requirements

Budgies enjoy a wide variety of foods and should be given more than just seeds in their diet. Remember, their native habitat is the arid central areas of Australia where they foraged for whatever seed, sprouted grasses, fruit and other foods and water they could find. Their efficient digestion system enables them to utilize every bit of nutrient available from the seeds they eat.

Seed alone does not provide the total vitamin and mineral requirements of these birds. Seed lacks the protein and has little of the required amino acid lysine and the vitamins A, D, B_2 (riboflavin), B_{12} and minerals such as calcium.

Since birds in captivity are absolutely dependent on you to assure they eat properly, it's important that you provide them with a healthy diet.

That may be easier said than done since all parrots, including budgies, have their likes and dislikes. They are creatures of habit and if they have been raised with one type of seed only, it may be difficult to coax them into eating fruits and vegetables. It's sort of like getting children to eat their vegetables—patience and ingenuity are required to introduce other foods that are good for them.

Budgerigar Seed

Commercially-prepared seed mixes for parakeets are available at most pet stores. These mixtures may contain any of several types of seeds such as Japanese millet, red

Facing page: A wide variety of bird foods and supplies is on hand at Birds of Paradise pet shop.

millet, canary, white millet, panicum millet, and hulled oats. The bird will select the type of seed it likes best from its food cup, disregarding or scattering the rest. Your bird will also appreciate millet sprays, which are available at most pet stores.

Generally, it is recommended that you buy seeds in see-through bags so you'll know that the seed is not bug-infested or has some other noticeable defect. Stay clear of seeds that smell moldy or that have lumps of seeds stuck together, indicating moisture in the bag that may have prompted the growth of a fungus that, if eaten, could prove fatal to your bird. The fresher the seeds the better, since the nutritional value of a seed diminishes with age.

Sprouted Seeds and Seed Grasses

One way of being sure you have fresh seeds is to sprout some. Since sprouted seeds and seeding grasses are nutritious treats for your budgie, these processes serve a dual purpose.

To sprout seeds, simply soak them for 24 hours in water. Drain and rinse them three times and then spread them on a clean towel, leaving them alone for another 24 hours until they just begin to sprout. Before giving the bird these sprouts, rinse them again thoroughly. Sprouts may be stored in the refrigerator for up to a week. There are commercial sprouters available, or you can do as I do—just buy some alfalfa or wheat sprouts at the grocery

Facing page, left: The swing and landing perch are just two examples of the many accessories especially designed for budgies. Right: Seeds, the principal budgie food, are not nutritionally adequate. Supplementary foods and vitamins are some of the items used to supply missing nutrients.

HAGEN®

WOODEN
BIRD SWING 3"

BALANÇOIR EN BOIS 3"
POUR OISEAUX

Petamine
THE WONDER FOOD
FOR CAGE BIRDS

NET WT. 32 OZS. (2 LBS.)
Kellogg Inc.

BIRD
LANDING
PERCH
WITH MIRROR
AND SEED CUP

ETHICAL PRODUCTS, INC.
SPOT PET DIV. NEWARK, N.J. 07105
© 1983 Ethical Products, Inc.   Made in Hong Kong

Lambert Kay
Avitron
Liquid Vitamin
Supplement

In Water
Soluble
Form

NET CONTENTS

store. Of course, this simple method does not help in determining the freshness of the seed purchased for the bird.

The birds also love young shoots of grasses grown from the seed. Madonna Stedman keeps a small flowerpot filled with grass shoots she grew by simply scattering some of the seeds into damp soil. Once the shoots appear, she just places the pot on the floor of the cage and all of her budgies flock to it.

When emptying my bird's seed cup, I sometimes sprinkle some of the leftover seed in a pot with some of my other plants. I add a little water and then forget about it until I see tiny grass shoots coming up, when I pick the grass—seed and all—and give it to my appreciative bird in her food dish.

Some bird fanciers use the little white paper candy cups available at some stores. With a little soil and seed, you'll have a steady supply of grass shoots available for your bird.

Sprouted and grass seeds are particularly important in the diet at times when birds need additional vitamins such as prior to and during breeding or molting.

In general, give your bird about a teaspoonful daily of seed sprouts and/or seed grasses, preferably in the early morning. A small amount of calcium carbonate or powdered cuttlebone may be added. If the bird appears to be gaining too much weight and is becoming too docile, cut back on this as well as on the more fattening seeds such as oats. If the bird appears to have diarrhea (runny droppings and a stained area around its vent), then stop the greens until the bird has recovered.

Facing page: Seeds may be sprouted in jars (1), or sown on the aviary floor and allowed to grow (2).

1▲

2▼

Fruits and Vegetables

It's amazing what a variety of foods a budgie will enjoy if given the chance. Try giving your bird small pieces of apples, pears, carrots, fresh corn on the cob, broccoli and romaine lettuce (not iceberg since that has very little nutritional value).

Also recommended is a tiny bit of cheese daily and a monkey biscuit either dry or soaked for 30 seconds in water or milk. Monkey biscuits are available from the pet store and are a great source of a variety of nutrients. The milk provides the needed lysine in the diet.

Remember, a bird will sometimes feel threatened by something new and different in its cage, but don't let this stop you from repeating the introduction of nutritious treats until the bird gets a taste of it. You can experiment with just about any foods, including meats. Just stay away from chocolate in pure form and pork products such as bacon.

Feeding Schedule

Your bird should be fed daily to assure the foods provided have not had time to spoil or be spoiled by the bird's droppings. Never leave fresh fruits and vegetables in the cage for longer than a day.

A seed dish may not have to be refilled on a daily basis, depending on the size and location of the dish. If it is protected from the bird's droppings and holds enough to feed the bird for a couple of days, then just be sure to daily stir the seeds up with your finger, blowing away the

Facing page: The plumage markings of this budgerigar show that it is a pied variety.

empty seed hulls on top. Don't be fooled into thinking the bird has plenty of seed when in fact there are just empty seed hulls.

A new bird may lose its appetite for a day or two as it adjusts to its new environment. Ordinarily, there is nothing to worry about. If the bird is not pestered and if a food supply is readily available the bird will eat. You might coax it to nourishment by sprinkling some of the seed on the floor of its cage. This practice should not be continued longer than necessary, however, since the food on the floor can be contaminated by the bird's droppings. Sometimes a bird will begin eating when it sees you eating.

If your bird refuses to eat after 24 hours have passed or if it begins to act sickly, call your veterinarian to see what he recommends.

And if a bird you've had for some time suddenly stops eating, then you may have cause to worry since a bird's high metabolic rate can lead to a rapid and fatal weight loss. These birds, used to searching for water in their wild state, are capable of going longer without water than without seed.

Watch for other behavioral changes in a bird that has lost its appetite. Contact your vet, who may ask you to bring him in. If the bird doesn't seem to be ill, an appetite stimulant may be recommended.

Natural Bark

Important trace elements and vitamins are available to your bird from chewing on branches and twigs, par-

Facing page, above: The variety called lutino is very different from the way budgerigars originally looked, typified by this green hen. Below: Birds are sensitive to changes in location; one can expect them to be temporarily off their food and lethargic after a move.

PAISLEY
& DISTRICT
BUDGERIGAR
SOCIETY

SPECIAL
AWARD

BUDGERIGA
nd BEST BEGINNER
/65

ticularly the bark and the buds of flowers and leaves. A plentiful supply of branches from willow, hazelnut, oak, maple, hibiscus or fruit trees is essential. Just be sure the branches have not been sprayed with insecticide and have been rinsed thoroughly before giving them to your feathered friend.

Necessary calcium can be provided in the form of a Nylabird toy available from a pet store or veterinarian or by the more traditional cuttlebone or calcium and mineral blocks.

Use of Vitamins

There are varying views on the inclusion of commercially prepared vitamins. Some bird fanciers recommend using soluble vitamins in the bird's drinking water and sprinkling a powdered vitamin supplement over fruits and vegetables. Others suggest adding the vitamins only during the cold winter months. As with humans, vitamins should not serve as an artificial replacement for a balanced diet. An overdose of vitamins can cause a great deal of damage, thus they should be administered with caution.

About Grit

Open almost any book on birds and there will be a section devoted to the necessity of grit in a bird's diet. Some bird fanciers believe the grit is necessary because it aids a bird's digestion, grinding and separating the seeds and

Overleaf: Prize-winning budgerigar in a show cage. Facing page: Medicines, nutritional toys, and dietary supplements—all are designed to meet particular budgerigar needs.

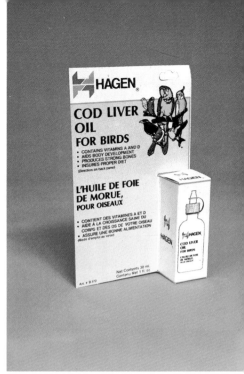

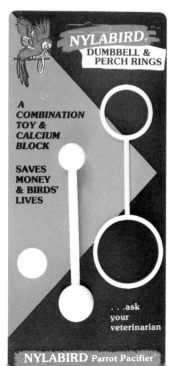

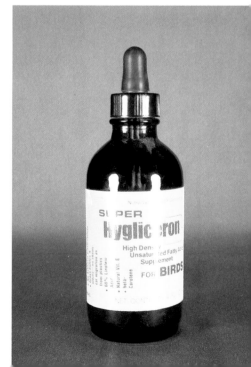

other foods as they pass through the gizzard. However, a more recent view held by some veterinarians is that grit can do more harm than good and, in fact, is not even necessary. The harm comes when a sick bird eats too much grit, resulting in death. If you do use grit, available at most pet stores, then make sure you remove it from the cage of an ill or injured bird. Because of the faith I have in Dr. Bush, I've followed his advice to not offer my birds grit and have had no problems.

Baby Bird Food

If your bird is a hand-fed infant, find out what the breeder gave it to eat and how long it's been weaned (never buy an unweaned infant). These babies may have additional nutritional requirements. There are various brands of prepared rearing foods available. Very young birds, as well as breeding birds and those recovering from illness, may require double feedings—twice the usual amount of food.

Keeping Your Bird Healthy

As with all parrots, a budgie will provide you with tremendous amounts of joy and satisfaction, asking only a minimum of care in return. Beyond providing it with a nutritious diet and a clean, safe environment, the follow-

Facing page: There are many sources of help when looking for the right information. Check with your local pet shop, a veterinarian, or a breeder, and make use of the many books available in pet shops and libraries.

ing tips should assure your pet has the healthiest lifestyle possible:

1) Make sure your bird has several hours of total darkness. Birds, like humans, need their rest. An artificial darkness from a covered cage, though better than nothing, does not allow a bird the total rest it needs.

There are mixed views on whether or not to keep your bird's cage covered at night. The bird is hardy by nature and is more inclined to catch cold from a lack of Vitamin A than from a draft, but if the bird seems to be stressed or slightly sick, covering the cage will help to keep it calm and warm. It will also enable the bird to rest more easily, especially during the daytime.

If the bird is being kept in an area where the lights are on the majority of the night, then by all means cover the cage to allow it some chance of rest. And if you have a cat or dog, the cover will provide protection from a nocturnal attack.

Covers can be made from a towel or cloth, or you can buy specially-made covers from the pet store.

2) The room temperature should be kept at a comfortable level—not too hot or too cold. Sudden drops of temperature should be avoided.

3) The cage should be cleaned daily. Just place a week's supply of papers on the bottom of the cage and each day remove the top layer to rid the cage of the bird's droppings. These droppings when dried can blow onto the bird's food and could cause illness. Paper towels and newspapers may be used as well as pre-cut papers found at the pet store.

Some stores recommend using chopped corn cob pieces (commercially available in some parts of the coun-

Facing page: The exhibition budgerigar, the result of generations of selective breeding, is larger and stockier than garden-variety budgies.

try) on the bottom of the cage since the soft, spongy substance is tremendously absorbent. Just by mixing it up daily, the soiled areas move to the bottom of the pile. Change the supply at least once a week.

Wash and dry the cage bottom and grill weekly with hot water and soap and sponge off cage bars periodically with plain water to keep the cage shiny and new-looking.

Change the bird's water daily, always washing the dish thoroughly with a brush, hot water and soap. Dirty water dishes are another source of disease for the bird. The seed cup should be washed thoroughly at least twice a week, more often if the bird has soiled it. Fresh seed should be provided daily. Under no circumstances allow day-old fruits, vegetables and other foods to remain in the cage.

Keep perches clean, using sand paper, a perch scraper or a paint scraper (available from your local hardware store). If you wash the perches, dry them completely before placing them back into a cage since a wet perch leads to colds and arthritic conditions. Natural perches should be replaced every few months.

4) Keep an eye out for infestations of mites and lice. If you feel your bird has external parasites, check for horizontal marks running across the heavy wing and tail feathers, an indication of lice. To check for mites, cover the cage with a white cloth at night. The tiny mites are attracted to the white cloth and will cling to it. Scaly leg mites, on the other hand, will show up in featherless areas of the bird such as the beak, legs and eyelids. These mites are hard to detect initially, but if left untreated will show up in small growths that will cover these entire areas.

Facing page, above: A perch scraper is a useful accessory. Below: Cups and dishes come in various sizes to fit the many different cages on the market.

Ordinarily, birds kept indoors will not have a parasitic problem, so don't worry too much about a bird that occasionally scratches, a natural part of their preening. Keeping the cage and bird clean will prevent a parasite problem from developing. As an extra precaution, however, there are some products available at pet stores that, when hung on the cage, discourage mites or lice. There also are some commercially prepared powders and scaly leg mite preparations that can be used on the bird and cage to rid them of infestation. Follow directions closely so as not to harm the bird.

5) Some budgies enjoy a bath, but it is basically a learned habit that comes from watching other birds in a bath. A gentle plant mister may be used to spray water on the bird, helping it to keep clean. There are some special bathing dishes available in pet stores.

6) When using pesticides in the house, remove the bird. Toxic fumes from insecticides, paints and the like can quickly overcome a bird. Too much cigarette smoke is also unhealthy.

7) When the bird undergoes molting—the normal change of plumage twice a year—its resistance to disease is strained. It is especially important at these times to make sure the bird's diet is rich in nutrients as outlined in the section on nutritional requirements.

Making Friends

If you've purchased a young bird with the intention of taming it, no doubt you're anxious to begin working with the bird as soon as you get it home.

Facing page: In becoming acquainted with a budgie, keep all movements slow and careful, so as not to frighten it.

Some bird enthusiasts recommend that you take advantage of the first hour the bird is home to make friends with it, capitalizing on the bird's disorientation and fear of the new environment. The argument is that if the bird is fearful, it may quickly come to depend on its human friend for safety. Proponents of this school of thought also recommend beginning the taming process as soon as possible so as not to lose valuable time. Remember, the younger the bird, the easier it will be to tame it. If you buy a bird that is more than six months old, valuable training time has been lost.

Others are more sensitive to the bird's fears, recommending that the new pet be given a day or two to get used to its new home. During this time the bird should be placed in an area where it can get used to seeing the person designated as the primary tamer. It should not be pestered by curious family members and friends. Make no sudden or frightening moves toward the bird during this critical time. This "quiet time" will enable it to get used to the normal household noises and routines.

A shy bird can be calmed by talking to it softly until it stops flying about the cage. By doing this often, the bird will soon remain on its perch when approached and may even respond with a soft chirping noise.

The birds are adaptable and hardy. After all, their short lives prior to being purchased are generally filled with upsetting changes — going from the nest to a cage filled with other birds and then to the life of a single, caged bird, totally isolated from its cohorts for the first time. But a little respect for their fears goes a long way toward winning a friend.

Facing page, above: Some budgies learn readily from speech-training tapes and records. Below: A heating pad is a handy source of warmth for budgies stressed by transport or illness.

Taming the Bird

Once the bird has settled in, it's time to start the taming process. In fact, this process begins the first time you talk softly to your bird. Once it gets used to your voice, it will sit quietly on its perch and appear to listen to you. It may even appear sleepy as if its eyes want to close.

You may win its trust more easily if you first provide it with some tidbits of treats such as greens or sprouted seeds through the bars of the cage. While it's eating, quietly open the cage door and slowly move your hand toward the bird. It may allow you to softly caress it, scratching its neck lightly with your finger.

Then slowly reach your hand toward the bird's chest. If the bird starts to move away, stop your hand's movement until the bird calms down again. Press the back of your hand gently against the bird's chest, causing it to be slightly off balance. This will force it to climb onto your hand.

Repeat this process over as many days as necessary to make the bird feel comfortable with its new owner. You may have better luck if you try this at night when the bird is calmer.

Once the bird is finger-tamed, you can slowly bring it through the open cage door. Make the first time out of the cage a short one, gradually lengthening the time until the bird is comfortable with its new home.

During the taming process, it is likely the bird will be startled and will fly away. Thus it is important to make sure all windows and doors are closed. To prevent possible injury, cover windows and mirrors until the bird learns the geography of the room.

Facing page: Many people favor a feather trim that does not leave the outermost primary feathers intact. Note that the primaries are cut just beyond the coverts that overlap them.

If the bird's wings haven't been clipped to impede flight, then the budgie will most likely seek a high spot on which to perch. Don't panic the bird by chasing after it or trying to bring it down with a broom or some other long object. Simply give the bird a few hours. When it gets hungry it will search for its food. Just make sure its cage with food is in clear view of the bird.

Fortunately for me, I am tall enough that I can reach up to most spots my bird flies to such as curtain rods and tops of bookcases. I simply repeat the process of placing my hand against its chest so that it must step on my hand. Then I slowly bring down my hand with the bird perched atop it.

After a few repeats of the whole taming process, the bird will soon have confidence in you and in its new home. Soon all you will have to do is open the cage door and the bird will come out, ready to perch on your finger. Most budgies enjoy riding on top of your head or on your shoulder. Some even like to tuck themselves under your hair.

If the bird is allowed to fly free, make sure all dangerous items are removed such as poisonous plants, uncovered windows, hot stoves and radiators and toxic items that the bird may chew on.

Clipping the Wings

To keep a bird from flying free or to make it easier to tame, some fanciers recommend clipping the bird's wing. This involves cutting some of the feathers on one or both of the wings.

Facing page: It should be no surprise that budgies prefer other budgies as companions, not people. Pet owners who find themselves unable to satisfy a single bird's need for companionship often purchase a second.

By clipping only one wing, the bird's flight is unbalanced because of its uneven wings. With this process, just cut the longest and last feathers on the wing. Clipping both wings allows the bird to fly for very short distances—more of a hopping flight. It is also more attractive. Just cut all but the last three feathers on each wing.

Most pet stores will clip your bird's wings before you take it home, but the procedure is easy enough for you to do yourself once you have seen it done. All you need is a light pair of good scissors and some Kwik Stop or hydrogen peroxide in case of bleeding.

Make sure you don't cut any blood feathers in the process. Blood feathers have not finished growing and thus have a blood vessel in the shaft to provide nourishment directly from the bird's vascular system. If a blood feather is accidentally clipped, stop the bleeding immediately since a budgie can bleed to death in a few minutes.

When cutting, hold the bird gently in one hand, using that hand to also hold the extended wing. Use your other hand to clip the feathers on the extended wing.

The clipped wing feathers will grow back only after the bird has molted. By that time the bird may be so tamed it may not be necessary to reclip the wings.

Training the Bird to Talk

Budgies have a wonderful reputation for easily learning a variety of words and phrases. One woman bragged that her parakeet knew at least 50 phrases, some of which

Facing page: In most cases, finger-taming a budgie is a necessary preliminary to any further training.

are lines from movies such as Clint Eastwood's "Make my day." Other birds have learned to say their owner's name and address, a helpful trick if the bird escapes and is found by a stranger.

The process can be time-consuming, however, taking as long as six months before the bird learns its first words. How quickly it takes to train a bird depends on the bird's capacity for learning and on your willingness to devote the time necessary on a regular basis.

When ready to begin training your bird, plan to spend a few minutes each day softly and distinctly repeating the same word, such as "Hello" or the bird's name. Work on only one new word at a time.

Choosing a training time early in the morning or late in the afternoon—its natural song time. To get the bird's total attention, cover half of the bird cage. It is also helpful if the bird is at eye level.

As you repeat the word, the bird will soon begin to cock its head as if listening to you. With time and persistence, the budgie will begin to repeat the word or words you've been saying to it. Once the bird mimics its first word, it will soon be picking up other words and phrases, some of which you may prefer it didn't learn. The bird can also mimic whistles using the same training process.

Some people who don't have the time or patience to spend with a bird leave the training to tapes or records that are available at pet stores. Others record their own voices, playing the tape back to the bird daily.

Don't overdo the lessons. Daily sessions for short periods of three to five minutes get better results than hours spent listening to your voice. A frustrated trainer who insists on overdoing the lessons will only prove stressful to your bird, who may have other ideas on how to spend his day.

Caring for the Sick or Injured Bird

An ounce of prevention goes a long way toward keeping your bird healthy and alive for the full lifespan of as long as 15 years.

As one vet said, it is unfortunately true that a bird is taken to a doctor only when it is sick. Instead, it should be checked annually by a qualified vet to assure the bird is healthy and that you are caring for it properly.

As with humans, even the best-cared for bird may acquire a disease or injury, so it's important to learn some of the symptoms of a sick bird.

The clever budgie instinctively will hide its sickness from you for as long as possible. This is because in the wild the sick, weak animals are those that fall victim to predators. So the parrot "fakes" normalcy for as long as possible. Though this may save its life in the wild, it may lead to its death in captivity, since a bird that is too sick to carry on this charade is often too sick to be helped, even by the best of veterinarians.

The better you learn your bird's habits, recognizing a change in pattern, the faster you'll be able to get medical attention if needed.

Common Warning Signs

Here are some common warning signs of possible illness:

1) A change in the bird's attitude, such as apathy and lethargy.
2) A change in the volume, texture and color of the bird's droppings (in a day's time, one bird should have about 20 droppings that should be black and white in color and of a fairly thick consistency, not runny).

3) A change in food and water consumption.
4) A change in the bird's appearance—ruffled feathers, runny eyes or nostrils, difficulty in maintaining its usual erect posture.
5) A change in the bird's activities—talking and whistling less than normal, little response to stimuli.
6) Difficulty in breathing, with respiratory sounds such as sneezing, wheezing or clicking.
7) Any noticeable enlargement on the bird's body—fat is abnormal on a bird.

If your bird exhibits any of these symptoms, it may be time to call a veterinarian for some advice. The doctor may recommend using some of the antibiotics available at the pet store or other remedies for colds and digestive disorders.

Hospital Cages

Because a sick bird is easily chilled, it will often respond to treatment in a heated "hospital cage." Specially-made hospital cages are available at pet stores, or you can turn your bird's cage into a care shelter by simply placing a heating pad on the top or bottom of the cage.

Turn the heating pad on to medium heat and cover most of the cage to keep in the warmth, allowing an area for fresh air to get through so that the bird has some choice as to where to sit to be most comfortable. This opening also allows the bird to keep an interest in what's happening outside of the cage. The temperature inside the cage should remain at about 85°F.

Some aviculturists recommend making a hospital cage using a low-wattage bulb and a rheostat so that the level of lighting can be adjusted to keep the temperature at the

Fluffed feathers, sitting low on the perch, and closed eyes may be signs of illness.

desired level. But others fear the brightness of the light prevents the bird from getting its needed rest. In fact, a sick bird, like a human, may need up to 16 hours of rest a day, with a mid-day nap thrown in for good measure, so keeping the bird in a darkened room to ensure quiet is advised.

All perches should be removed and the food dishes placed on the floor in easy reach of the bird.

In cases where the budgie has stopped eating, place a spray of millet on the floor of the cage. Millet is easily digested by birds and is a favorite of budgies. This is especially recommended for a bird suffering from a gastro-intestinal problem that is keeping it from digesting its food normally.

When to See a Vet

If your bird fails to respond fairly quickly to these measures, then take the bird to a vet. A sick bird fails rapidly and there is little time to waste in seeking treatment.

An injury that causes bleeding should also be quickly cared for since the bird has little blood in its vascular system and can quickly bleed to death. Pack the bleeding area with Kwik Stop or use hydrogen peroxide. If first aid medication is not readily available, baking flour helps stop the bleeding.

In some cases, stitches may be required or a broken bone must be set, both procedures that should be done by a vet or an experienced bird fancier. If an injury results in the amputation of an appendage, the bird will likely adjust to its new limitations as long as you protect it from predators who might take advantage of its handicap.

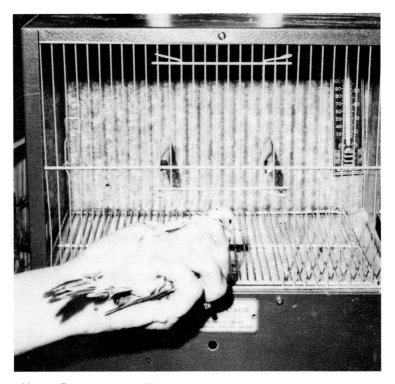

Above: Because many illnesses prevent birds from maintaining body temperature, the hospital cage has saved many lives. Below: The eyedropper is one of the ways medicine can be administered.

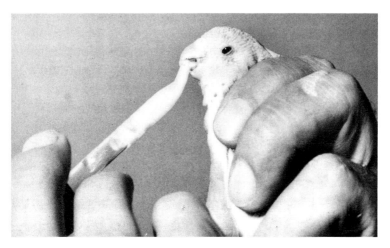

When Tweetie Bird was injured by my dog, its foot was broken. After calming the bird down by gently holding it in my hands close to my body, I called my vet, who advised me to bring the bird in immediately. He kept Tweetie for two days in a hospital cage. The first 24 hours, he said, were the most critical since the stress of the experience of being "played" with by a dog could cause death. After a day in the warmth of the quiet hospital cage, the bird was ready to have its leg set with a special splinting tape.

The doctor advised me to remove all perches from Tweetie's cage to prevent it from climbing with its splinted foot. Food was to be kept on the floor in easy reach. He even suggested using a square or rectangle aquarium instead of the cage since the smooth glass sides would force the bird to remain quietly on the cage bottom, preventing further injury. After 21 days, Tweetie's leg was as good as new.

Diseases

A sick bird may be suffering from any of several diseases and conditions known to affect budgies. Some diseases affect the bird's respiratory system causing bronchitis or pneumonia. Others affect the gastro-intestinal system, causing it to regurgitate its seed grains.

Psittacosis

The most dreaded disease feared by all bird lovers is psittacosis (parrot disease). More correctly it should be called ornithosis (bird disease), since it is not limited to

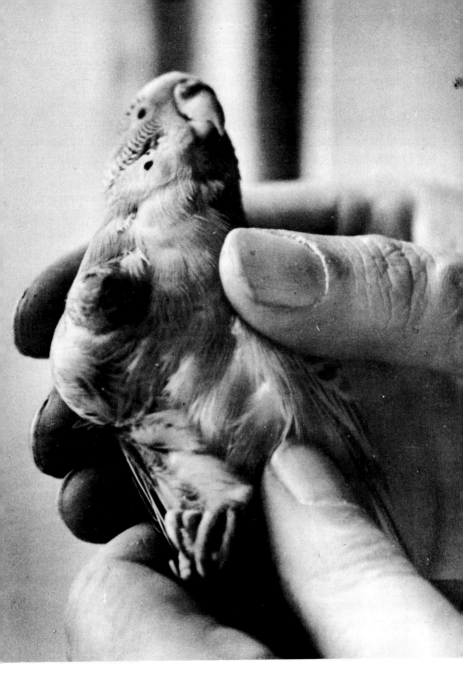

Examining your pet regularly helps to detect illness before it becomes serious.

the parrot family. This disease can be transmitted to man, manifesting itself as a flu-like illness that has been known to cause death. However, medical advances in antibiotics for both bird and man have made it a curable disease and it is no longer necessary to destroy entire collections of birds as in the past. Psittacosis is difficult to diagnose in birds since symptoms such as excessive sleepiness, diarrhea or pneumonia among birds are observed only in cases of very severe infection. But any bird breeder who has a high rate of mortality should have the dead birds examined. If psittacosis is diagnosed, the authorities must be notified to prevent the disease from spreading to other bird colonies.

Clipping the Claws

A budgie allowed to fly about the house may do some damage not only to the furnishings but to itself if its claws are allowed to grow. The bird injures itself when its claws get caught by fabric or something similar just as it's about to take flight.

By providing the bird with natural wooden perches this should not be much of a problem. If, however, the claws become overgrown to the point of curling, they should be clipped cautiously with great care taken to avoid cutting the vein within the toe.

The claw clipping procedure should be done in a good light so that the blood vessels in the claws can be easily seen. Hold the bird firmly but gently in one hand, isolating a foot with the fingers of that hand. Use the other hand to trim the claws. Remember that it is better to leave the claw too long than to cut it too close to the blood vessel, thus taking the risk of the bird bleeding to death. Don't forget to have some Kwik Stop or hydrogen peroxide on hand to stop any bleeding.

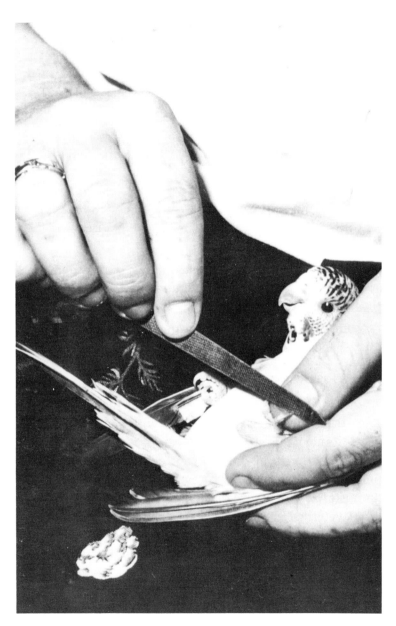

Usually the need for claw clipping increases as a budgie ages and becomes less active. In this instance, however, a youngster is having its claws dulled to make finger-taming more pleasant for the owner.

Colds

Just as humans have colds, so do birds. The symptoms are even similar, including a runny nose, sneezing, apathy, lack of appetite, difficulty in breathing and watery eyes.

If your bird shows these symptoms, isolate it from any other bird and place it in a hospital cage where it will be kept warm. Make sure the bird doesn't stop eating, feeding it special treats such as a millet spray. In sóme cases medication available at pet stores will help the bird or else a veterinarian can recommend the proper treatment if the bird fails to respond to treatment.

If the cold develops into pneumonia, an antibiotic must be given to the bird in addition to the treatment outlined for a cold.

Sour Crop

An irritated crop, the area where a bird's food is stored before digestion, can cause problems with a bird's eating habits. It may regurgitate what it eats or it may not eat at all, thus the need for quick action. Usually a drop of a commercially available antibiotic known as tetracycline administered with an eye dropper will clear up the problem. A veterinarian may also recommend giving the bird a drop of mineral oil.

For detailed descriptions of the various illnesses and conditions that can harm a budgie, I suggest buying *Bird Diseases* by Heinz-Sigurd Raethel.

In the disease known as French molt, the feathers grow poorly and are easily damaged.

Other Health Problems

Health problems caused by a dirty environment can be easily prevented by regular cleaning of the cage bottom and aviary floor, with disinfecting recommended at least twice a year. Without cleaning, mites, bacteria and parasitic worms proliferate, potentially harming your pet.

Nutritional deficiencies can cause health problems such as French molt or "runner's disease." The nickname comes from the fact that a bird with French molt loses its feathers, preventing it from flying from its enemies. Instead, it runs away from predators. In most cases, with the proper diet of increased amino acid preparations and vitamins, the bird's feathers will eventually grow back. In those cases where the feather loss is permanent, it is advisable to have the bird put to sleep.

Beak Trimming

In cages with the proper wooden perches, Nylabird and cuttlebone or mineral blocks, the bird's beak should not need to be trimmed. If, however, the bird's beak does begin to interfere with normal eating, it should be carefully trimmed on all three sides. Nail clippers may be used. If the problem is only a slight one, it may be filed with a nail file.

To clip or file the beak, the bird's head should be gently held between the thumb and index finger. The bird may be kept from biting during the procedure by inserting a small twig between the upper and lower mandible and allowing the bird to bite down. Before filing, rub the mandible (beak) with cooking oil to keep it from splintering or tearing.

Mite infestation has produced the beak deformity shown here.

Dealing with a Dead Bird

Sometimes, no matter how well you care for your bird, your budgie will succumb to age, disease or injury.

If you have other birds and fear that a contagious disease caused the death, it would be wise to take the dead bird with a sample of its droppings to a veterinarian. The vet can determine the cause of death.

In homes where children have come to love the bird, its death can cause a great upset. As with other types of pets, the loss of your bird may prompt your youngster to ask questions about death. This may be a good opportunity to explain your own views of death, taking care to provide simple answers that address only what the child has asked—no more and no less. How you handle your bird's death will help pattern your child's means of dealing with the inevitable loss of loved ones throughout his or her life.

If the youngster would like to bury the bird, simply find a sturdy box to place it in. Let the child decide where the bird should be buried and then proceed with the service, allowing the child to determine as much as possible how the funeral should be conducted.

If no children are involved and there is no sentimentality attached to the loss of the bird or no need to have a veterinarian establish the cause of death, its body may be wrapped in newspapers or similar material and placed in the trash or incinerator for disposal.

Breeding Your Budgie

A major reason for the budgie's success as the most popular parrot-family bird in the world is its ability to breed in captivity. In fact, when these little birds were first brought to Europe over 100 years ago, breeders did just about everything wrong according to what we know today, and the birds still proved to be prolific breeders.

However, if you buy one pair of budgies in hopes of being a successful bird breeder, you may be in for some disappointment. Although a single pair has been known to breed in captivity, it is against the nature of this colony or community bird that instinctively wants the protection of other breeding birds nearby.

"I've had very little luck in getting a pair to breed by themselves," said pet store owner John Smithers. "But when I take a pair that has been kept isolated and then place them in a room—not necessarily in the same cage—with other birds, the budgies breed."

So if you want to have baby budgies, you may have to invest in a larger cage or an aviary in order to accommodate a variety of birds. If you want to assure that certain budgies breed, then the selected pair will have to be kept in a separate cage or portion of the aviary.

If it doesn't matter which birds mate, then colony breeding—all the budgies in a single cage or aviary—is acceptable. The birds will pair up on their own with each pair selecting its own nest box from the variety you've provided.

Selecting Your Breeding Pair

The most important factor in breeding budgies is

selecting healthy birds to mate. The same criteria followed in selecting your single caged bird should be followed with every budgie obtained.

Making sure your birds have the properly balanced diet as outlined in the section on nutrition is critical for birds about to enter the breeding cycle since this reproductive process puts a strain on the bird's health.

Birds breeding for the first time should preferably be a year old, though some birds are mature enough after nine months.

When introducing pairs, some bird fanciers such as John Smithers recommend giving them a few days to adjust to each other before offering the nesting box. Others suggest making the nesting box available from the start. If either of the birds harms the other or acts overly aggressive, or if mating does not take place after several weeks, then separate them and try another partner. Not all matches are made in heaven!

Breeding for Color

If you are breeding your birds strictly for hobby with no care for producing a particular variety of the many-colored type birds, then the color of the birds selected for mating will not matter. It is also not necessary to separate each mating pair, breeding them instead in a "colony" type arrangement.

If, however, you intend to exhibit your birds or are interested in a particular color, then careful consideration must be given to the color and the physical characteristics of the mated pair. A study of genetics would be in order to determine what types of matches result in the colors of birds preferred.

For example, if I bred a lutino (yellow) cock with a

The young budgies shown earlier in this book are now mostly
feathered in.

lutino hen, the offspring would be lutino. If, however, I mated that lutino cock with a green hen, the lutino characteristic would only be passed on to the female offspring.

As a general rule of thumb, the light colors are primarily recessive and are dominated by darker colors. There are two main color categories—the blue series and the green series. If you breed like-colored birds, such as two greens or two blues, then you'll most likely get offspring resembling the parents. If you breed together one of each series, you will get offspring with more intensely colored feathers.

However, to ensure a hardy generation of budgies, breeders prefer to use the green series. Even when breeding for blue variations, a breeder will use a green with some blue in its lineage to mate with a blue since the greens are generally stronger birds.

Some of the varieties of the green series include dark-green, olive-green, gray-green, opaline green, cinnamon, opaline cinnamon-gray-green, lace wings and the pieds or "harlequins."

The blue series does not have the yellow pigments, thus the feathers that are colored yellow in the green series are white in the blue series. Markings are black and white instead of black and yellow and the base feathers are light blue instead of light green, dark blue instead of dark green, mauve instead of olive-green and gray instead of gray-green.

The information on breeding specific color variations provided above is meant more for the hobbyist than for the professional breeder. For more detailed information on breeding, genetics and exhibition of show birds, I recommend purchasing *Encyclopedia of Budgerigars* by Georg A. Radtke.

When to Breed

Since budgerigars are by nature opportunistic breeders, meaning they breed when conditions are right, you can control their breeding cycle by providing or taking away the nest boxes. In captivity, a typical breeding season is between August and December, with some birds successfully mating as early as April. Often breeders will foster mating in October in order to have plenty of babies available for Christmas gifts. In warmer climates such as Florida or Hawaii, the pairs are often separated during the hot summer months when temperatures in nesting boxes can get extremely high.

Budgies may successfully breed for about four years if properly cared for. It is recommended they be allowed to breed successively only twice a year.

The Nest Box

Whether breeding takes place in a cage or aviary, nest boxes must be provided for the hen to lay her eggs. These nest boxes are usually made from plywood and are usually about 8 inches wide and 10 inches high with an entrance hole 2 inches in diameter at one end.

In a colony situation there should be more nest boxes available than there are breeding pairs to allow each hen a chance to select the box she prefers. The boxes may be slightly different.

Nesting boxes made especially for budgies are available at most pet stores. Some are made to be attached to the inside of the cage while others are attached to the outside of the cage. The latter doesn't take up any of the flight space in the cage itself.

It is important that the box have a means of allowing

the breeder to check on the hen and her eggs through either a side or top door. Smithers makes sure the door has a hook or screw in it to prevent the gregarious bird on the inside from trying to escape. There should be several small holes near the top of the box for ventilation.

The inside bottom of the box must be slightly concave to keep the eggs from rolling around. Though not necessary, fine sawdust may be added to the nest.

Courtship and Mating

Once the nest boxes are hung, the budgies will embark on their courtship. Both birds should actively fly about the cage. When they land on a perch, they will seemingly exercise their wings without flying.

The cere of the cock ready for mating will be shiny blue except on birds that are lutinos, albinos, fallows, lacewings or recessive pieds. The cere on these birds will be a fleshy purple color. The hen's cere will be a chocolate brown.

The male will beat against the perch and the cage walls with his beak and will jump up and down on the perch next to the female. Once the female becomes excited, she, too, will join in this dance. The pupils of both birds will contract and their irises will become larger. She may want to be fed by the cock, and he will comply by regurgitating food from his crop. Both will be singing and chattering to each other.

When finally ready, the female will drop her wings and raise her tail, enabling the male to mount her. The male, sliding one wing around the female and hanging onto the female's back with his claws and beak, will slide downward for copulation.

A flying budgerigar about to land on a perch.

Eggs

After mating, the hen will begin staying for longer periods in the confines of her nest. The bird's abdominal area will become increasingly swollen, and within eight to 14 days after mating, the first egg is laid. If this is the first time a hen has bred, it may take as long as four weeks for her to lay her first egg.

The remaining eggs—as many as eight altogether—are generally laid every two days, with incubation lasting from 18 to 20 days. The first egg laid will be the first to hatch, with its siblings following suit in two-day intervals.

Hatched Nestlings

The newly hatched birds are fed the first few days with a secretion of predigested foods produced by the female. The female can vary the diet of the nestlings according to their age: the newly-hatched nestling receives this stomach milk, while the older birds receive mucus-coated seeds from the female's crop.

The female is fed by the male so that she may remain with the nestlings, keeping them warm by covering them with her body and wings. If the male does not provide her with enough food, she may gather her own.

To make it easier for the parent birds to feed the young, it is suggested that their diet be supplemented with germinating seeds (as discussed in the section on nutrition) and soft foods such as those purchased from a pet store. You can make your own soft food using whole wheat bread and ground-up hard-boiled egg moistened by one finely ground carrot.

Throughout incubation and the early days of the nest-

The chick's down coat is replaced by contour feathers, of which the larger ones are the first to appear.

ling's life, it is important to make daily checks on the nest to assure that the female's hasn't harmed either her eggs or her offspring.

If the nestling continuously chirps after hatching, indicating that it is not being fed properly, transfer it to the nest of another breeding female. If that is not possible, hand-feeding may become necessary. There are several commercially available nestling foods on the market that may be administered to a newborn bird with an eye dropper several times daily. Without food, the nestling will die within 12 hours.

The infant bird is not a pretty sight. The tiny nestling has no feathers and depends totally on its mother for warmth. It is nearly blind. Within eight days it is beginning to look like a bird, with its fluffy down cover that is gray in normal-colored budgies and white in the lighter-colored varieties. After two weeks, the regular colored feathers will appear, and after another week the birds look like budgies.

The nestlings leave their nests sometime between the fourth and fifth weeks. Prior to "take off," the sound of their wings fluttering in practice can be heard inside the nest box walls. The oldest bird is usually the first to approach the nest box entrance. Once it has flown outside of its nest, it rarely returns.

After leaving the nest, the young birds will eat the seeds provided the older birds, but the male will continue to supplement their diet for as long as two weeks, gradually decreasing the amount given.

The female pays no attention to her young once they've left the nest. In fact, she may already be caring for a new clutch of eggs. This probably won't cause any problems unless there are stragglers from the first hatch that aren't quite ready to leave the nest. She may "kick them out" anyway, possibly causing injury to the young birds.

The new eggs may be dirtied by the waste of the first hatch. In this case, the breeder can carefully wash the eggs in lukewarm water.

If the aviary or cage is large enough, the addition of the young birds will not cause a problem. However, the new birds can be removed at about six weeks of age, a perfect time to begin taming them to make them perfect pets for new owners.

After the second (and sometimes third) brood has left the nest, the nest box should be taken down. The female may be removed to another cage, but the male should be allowed to stay in the same cage with the youngest birds until they are totally independent.

Exhibiting Birds

As mentioned previously, starting out with one caged budgie may open up a world that includes breeding these marvelous creatures. Once that step is taken, it's an easy jump to breeding for particular color variations and on to birds with the physical characteristics necessary to do well in exhibitions.

If you reach this point, then it behooves you to learn the rules and standards of the cage bird or budgerigar society in your area. Such standards vary from state to state and country to country.

In large cities there should be access to organizations that sponsor bird shows on a regular basis. You can usually find these groups by checking with a veterinarian or pet store in the area or by checking the telephone directory and newspaper classified advertisements.

The following guidelines are the general qualities desired in a show bird:

1) The bird must be in good health, not underweight or overweight or out of condition.

2) The bird must have a balanced appearance while on its perch, with its body aligned with its head, angled toward an 11 or 1 o'clock position.

3) There must be six rounded, evenly spaced throat spots on a wide mask along with a wide cheek patch.

4) The neck should not be overly long or short but in good proportion so that the head and body are in alignment.

5) The bird should be about 8½ inches from the tip of the head to the end of the tail.

6) The tail should be long enough to give the bird a balanced appearance.

7) The legs and feet should be straight and capable of supporting the bird's weight.

8) The wings should fold neatly against the body.

Judging will also be based on color variations, with judges looking for bright, well-defined colors on the feathers, mask, cap and throat spots.

Even if you don't want to show your bird competitively, attending bird exhibitions provides an excellent opportunity to learn about the various breeding techniques and the latest findings in genetics research. By talking with the breeders and bird fanciers you'll have a wonderful opportunity to obtain general information on successfully caring for these precious little birds.

Conclusion

I hope the information provided in these pages will be helpful to you in caring for your budgie. Researching this book and talking with those knowledgeable about the caring and breeding of the budgies have been a tremendous learning experience.

I've included some of my personal experiences and ordeals with Tweetie, who did recover from her unfortunate encounter with my dog. Her survival was due in large part to the advice provided me by the bird enthusiasts who helped me in writing this book. I hope their expertise will provide you with assistance when you need it as well.

As mentioned in the introduction, parakeets had little appeal for me until I began researching this book. But after acquiring Tweetie and watching other bird owners with their budgies, it soon became apparent why these precious creatures have become one of the world's favorite cage birds.

If you are fortunate enough to have a budgie for a companion, take care of it, learn its habits and respect its individuality so that you may have the joy this creature is sure to provide you with for many years.

Index